ALA Survey of Librarian Salaries 2003

Mary Jo Lynch, *Project Director*

ALA Survey Report

American Library Association
Office of Research and Statistics

American Library Association
Chicago 2003

ISBN 0-8389-8227-1

ISSN 0747-7201

Copyright © 2003 by the American Library Association.
All rights reserved except those which may be granted by Sections 107 and 108 of the Copyright Revision Act of 1976.

Printed in the United States of America.

Acknowledgments

Thanks are due to the many respondents who completed our questionnaires. Without their cooperation, this report would not be possible. We are grateful to the Association of Research Libraries (ARL) for sharing data with us as described in Appendix C and especially to Martha Kyrillidou, ARL Senior Program Officer for Statistics and Measurement, who sent the data electronically. We are also grateful to Ed Lakner, Diane LaBarbera, Lidan Luo, Anita Michel, and other staff at the Library Research Center of the Graduate School of Library and Information Science at the University of Illinois who managed the mailings and processed the returns. Appendix A was prepared by Maxine Moore, Program Officer in ALA's Office for Human Resource Development and Recruitment. Finally, thanks are due to Kathy Bork, Administrative Assistant in the Office for Research and Statistics (ORS) for word processing the revised text and tables.

Table of Contents

Acknowledgements iii

Introduction 1

Results 3

Director/Dean 4
Deputy/Associate/Assistant Directors 7
Department Heads/Coordinators/Senior Managers 10
Managers/Supervisors of Support Staff 13
Librarians who do not supervise 16
Beginning Librarians 19

Discussion

Summary of Results 22
    Salaries by Type of Position 22
    Salaries by Type of Library 22
    Salaries by Region of the U.S. 23
    Problem with Categories New in 1999 23

Complicating Factors 23
    Meaning of "Full-Time" 23
    Meaning of "Professional" 23
    Salaries Below $22,000 23
    Job Levels or Faculty Ranks 24
    Level of Experience 24

Appendixes

A. Compensation Surveys Providing Information on Library Workers 25
B. ALA Policies Relating to Compensation Issues 32
C. Technical Considerations 35
D. Cover Letters 40
E. Survey Questionnaire 43
F. Salaries Paid for Less than a 12-month Year in Academic Libraries 47

Introduction

Librarians, the people who hire them, and interested others often ask the American Library Association (ALA) to tell them what salary might be paid to a librarian in a particular type of position, working in a particular type of library, in a particular part of the U.S. To fill the need for information of this kind, ALA began conducting a periodic survey of salaries for full-time professionals in academic and public libraries. Reports were published biennially from 1982 to 1988 and became annual in 1989.

This report, the nineteenth in a series, is similar to its predecessors in many ways but different in one important way, which is described at the end of this Introduction. Otherwise, the 2003 report shares the following characteristics with its predecessors:

- It is based on salaries paid as of April 1st of the survey year.

- It is based on a survey of **libraries**, not individual librarians.

- It is based on a survey of **full-time** positions.

- It is based on a survey of **public and academic** libraries only. (Sources for salaries in other libraries are given in Appendix A.)

- It is based on a survey of libraries with at least **two professionals**. (See Appendix C for how this term is defined for public libraries and for academic libraries.)

- The public and academic library universe is stratified by the same **type/size criteria**: public libraries serving populations of from 25,000 to 99,999, public libraries serving populations of 100,000 or more, two-year colleges, four-year colleges, and universities. (The last category includes all institutions offering work beyond the bachelor's level).

- The nation is stratified into the same **geographic areas**: North Atlantic, Great Lakes and Plains, Southeast, West and Southwest (see Appendix C for list of states).

- It shows the **first quartile, median, and third quartile** for salaries paid in each type/size of library and region in addition to the **mean and range** (low and high) for each position reported.

- It shows salaries paid to staff **with master's degrees from programs in library and information studies accredited by ALA**.

- It shows salaries for **beginning librarians** in both public and academic libraries.

In the 1999 report, there was a change in how positions were described. Since the beginning, the ALA survey has collected salary data on staff holding three administrative positions (director, deputy/associate/assistant director, department/branch head) and three positions described in terms of content of work (reference/information librarian, cataloger/classifier, children's/young adult librarian). For 1999, the top two administrative positions remained and all other positions were collapsed into three, which focus on the nature of responsibility for the work of other staff: Department Heads/Coordinators/Senior Managers, Managers/Supervisors of Support Staff, and Librarians who do not supervise. This 2003 report used those same categories.

The changes were made for the following reasons:

1. The personnel systems in many libraries are not set up to provide the kind of information we were

requesting (i.e., by position title related to job content).

2. Recent technological developments have led to the creation of many new positions in libraries. Although the titles are not standardized enough to warrant use in a survey instrument, without the salaries paid to staff in those positions, the results would not adequately represent the reality of the job market.

The Library Research Center of the University of Illinois Graduate School of Library and Information Science performed the mailing, processing, and computer analysis of the questionnaires. Mary Jo Lynch, Director of ALA's Office for Research and Statistics (ORS), directed the project and wrote this report.

Note: Since 1994, this annual salary survey has included unique "Supplementary Questions" which gathered information on an issue related to library personnel. For 2003, the questions were as follows:

Please circle the appropriate code numbers below to indicate what benefits your library provides and which staff are eligible. Use your own definitions of full-time and part-time. Do not report benefits that are for the director only as determined by contract negotiations.

	Professional Staff		Support Staff		Not provided
	Full-time	Part-time	Full-time	Part-time	
Health insurance	1	2	3	4	5
Dental insurance	1	2	3	4	5
Life insurance	1	2	3	4	5
Vision insurance	1	2	3	4	5
Disability insurance	1	2	3	4	5
Prescription insurance	1	2	3	4	5
Health insurance	1	2	3	4	5
Dental insurance	1	2	3	4	5
Vacation	1	2	3	4	5
Sick leave	1	2	3	4	5
Personal days	1	2	3	4	5
Bereavement leave	1	2	3	4	5
Pension	1	2	3	4	5
Retirement savings	1	2	3	4	5
Vacation	1	2	3	4	5
Sick leave	1	2	3	4	5
Training & education	1	2	3	4	5
Tuition reimbursement	1	2	3	4	5
Credit union	1	2	3	4	5
Professional memberships	1	2	3	4	5
Transportation subsidies	1	2	3	4	5
Child care	1	2	3	4	5
Elder care	1	2	3	4	5
Long-term care	1	2	3	4	5

Other (*please specify benefit & circle appropriate codes*)

_____	1	2	3	4	
_____	1	2	3	4	

Results will be compiled and released before the end of 2003. A notice of availability will be widely distributed or you can contact ORS at ors@ala.org.

Results

The survey questionnaire was mailed to 1,268 randomly selected libraries on April 11, 2003. Samples were drawn from twenty groups of libraries formed by stratifying five type-of-library categories by four regions of the U. S. Appendix D describes how groups were formed and sampled. By the end of June, usable responses had been received from 901 libraries, 71.1 percent of those sampled.

The results of this survey are presented on the following pages in six sets of tables. There are three pages of tables for each position. The first table presents salaries paid in medium-sized public libraries, i.e., those serving between 25,000 and 99,999. For each of four regions of the country and for the nation as a whole, the table shows the number of positions reported (N), the lowest salary and the highest salary (range), the mean (arithmetic average), the first quartile, median, and third quartile. This pattern is repeated for large public libraries (i.e., those serving populations of 100,000 or more), and for libraries in two-year colleges, four-year colleges, and in universities (i.e., institutions offering work beyond the baccalaureate degree).

The following example illustrates how to interpret the tables. In the first table for the position of director--the table presenting salaries paid in medium-sized public libraries--there were 78 salaries reported from the North Atlantic region. The lowest of these was $24,000 and the highest was $141,500. When all the salaries were added together and the result was divided by the total number (78) the average or mean was $73,865. When all the salaries were arrayed from low to high, 25 percent of them fell below $59,938, the first quartile, 50 percent fell below $70,356, the median, and 50 percent were above $70,356. Seventy-five percent fell below $85,881, the third quartile, and 25 percent were above that amount. The middle 50 percent of the salaries fell between $59,938 and $85,881.

Two caveats should be observed in reading the tables. The higher the number of cases (N), the more reliable the results of the sample in giving a true picture of the total population. When the number of cases is less than twenty-five, the results should be used with caution. This caution is especially applicable to the regional data for libraries where the number of professional staff is often small--medium sized public libraries, four-year colleges, and two-year colleges. Another caveat is that when the mean and the median are not close together, the mean is being influenced by some unusual values. When the mean is much higher than the median, there are several very high salaries. When the mean is much lower than the median, there are several very low salaries.

DIRECTOR/DEAN
(Page 1 of 3)

Chief officer of the library or library system

Medium-sized Public Library
(Serving a population of from 25,000 to 99,999)

	Mean	First Quartile	Median	Third Quartile
North Atlantic N = 78 Range = $24,000 - $141,500	73,865	59,938	70,356	85,881
Great Lakes & Plains N = 80 Range = $39,859 - $120,060	70,855	57,094	71,192	80,480
Southeast N = 51 Range = $37,416 - $87,192	56,228	46,061	55,000	62,471
West & Southwest N = 51 Range = $40,000 - $138,338	78,599	59,948	75,000	95,630
All Regions N = 260 Range = $24,000 - $141,500	70,408	56,074	67,150	80,000

Large Public Library
(Serving a population of 100,000 or more)

	Mean	First Quartile	Median	Third Quartile
North Atlantic N = 41 Range = $57,200 - $225,000	98,420	75,084	89,258	115,199
Great Lakes & Plains N = 48 Range = $46,738 - $145,513	94,883	78,859	88,719	110,798
Southeast N = 51 Range = $54,042 - $156,840	92,822	74,381	88,000	111,000
West & Southwest N = 66 Range = $43,201 - $190,843	105,034	86,728	104,960	121,519
All Regions N = 206 Range = $43,201 - $225,000	98,329	78,663	94,515	115,436

Source: ALA Survey of Librarian Salaries, 2003

Director/Dean (Page 2 of 3)

Chief officer of the library or library system

Two-Year College

	Mean	First Quartile	Median	Third Quartile
North Atlantic N = 31 Range = $32,067 - $102,000	70,016	52,000	71,000	85,000
Great Lakes & Plains N = 26 Range = $25,000 - $88,580	59,448	43,553	57,112	78,948
Southeast N = 33 Range = $27,800 - $98,438	58,708	51,530	57,012	62,607
West & Southwest N = 28 Range = $38,900 - $128,337	59,340	46,650	57,164	70,150
All Regions N = 118 Range = $25,000 - $128,337	61,992	49,700	58,088	74,167

Four-Year College

	Mean	First Quartile	Median	Third Quartile
North Atlantic N = 25 Range = $41,000 - $112,000	61,530	51,000	57,450	63,500
Great Lakes & Plains N = 30 Range = $36,000 - $104,000	57,388	42,750	53,037	65,767
Southeast N = 23 Range = $34,000 - $114,966	59,403	45,000	52,000	75,000
West & Southwest N = 30 Range = $31,000 - $111,510	60,843	47,383	56,891	75,198
All Regions N = 108 Range = $31,000 - $114,966	59,736	47,148	54,987	70,863

Source: ALA Survey of Librarian Salaries, 2003

Director/Dean (Page 3 of 3)

Chief officer of the library or library system

University

	Mean	First Quartile	Median	Third Quartile
North Atlantic N = 35 Range = $41,240 - $276,500	94,494	65,000	84,801	105,000
Great Lakes & Plains N = 40 Range = $53,040 - $193,640	102,101	74,025	98,500	123,671
Southeast N = 37 Range = $38,700 - $180,000	87,999	62,315	82,462	107,837
West & Southwest N = 37 Range = $51,000 - $241,280	102,355	80,960	100,000	123,502
All Regions N = 149 Range = $38,700 - $276,500	96,875	71,608	92,925	112,542

All Academic and Public Libraries

	Mean	First Quartile	Median	Third Quartile
North Atlantic N = 210 Range = $24,000 - $276,500	80,061	59,588	74,053	94,069
Great Lakes & Plains N = 224 Range = $25,000 - $193,640	78,456	57,338	73,975	93,410
Southeast N = 195 Range = $27,800 - $180,000	72,621	52,908	64,896	85,930
West & Southwest N = 212 Range = $31,000 - $241,280	85,919	60,250	81,535	106,231
All Regions N = 841 Range = $24,000 - $276,500	79,385	57,437	74,106	95,815

Source: ALA Survey of Librarian Salaries, 2003

DEPUTY/ASSOCIATE/ASSISTANT DIRECTORS
(Page 1 of 3)

Persons who report to the Director and manage major aspects of the library operation. (e.g., technical services, public services, collection development, systems/automation)

Medium-sized Public Library
(Serving a population of from 25,000 to 99, 999)

	Mean	First Quartile	Median	Third Quartile
North Atlantic N = 60 Range = $29,870 - $88,961	60,365	49,849	59,576	70,604
Great Lakes & Plains N = 94 Range = $25,189 - $75,825	49,227	39,807	47,810	58,627
Southeast N = 57 Range = $22,000 - $65,224	39,850	32,000	39,000	45,328
West & Southwest N = 36 Range = $30,406 - $93,225	57,374	45,004	50,149	71,934
All Regions N = 247 Range = $22,000 - $93,225	50,956	39,319	49,051	60,937

Large Public Library
(Serving a population of 100,000 or more)

	Mean	First Quartile	Median	Third Quartile
North Atlantic N = 133 Range = $24,500 - $157,500	75,547	55,133	71,925	88,291
Great Lakes & Plains N = 131 Range = $38,649 - $126,674	71,522	57,943	67,808	85,000
Southeast N = 120 Range = $25,700 - $110,885	65,333	51,060	65,967	78,004
West & Southwest N = 156 Range = $28,289 - $129,334	74,076	59,038	72,779	91,983
All Regions N = 540 Range = $24,500 - $157,500	71,876	56,599	69,999	85,448

Source: ALA Survey of Librarian Salaries, 2003

Deputy/Associate/Assistant Directors (Page 2 of 3)

Persons who report to the Director and manage major aspects of the library operation. (e.g., technical services, public services, collection development, systems/automation)

Two-Year College

	Mean	First Quartile	Median	Third Quartile
North Atlantic N = 20 Range = $33,109 - $79,000	57,289	42,734	58,427	69,900
Great Lakes & Plains N = 12 Range = $33,000 - $122,667	55,022	33,047	42,250	61,875
Southeast N = 14 Range = $22,745 - $73,937	43,709	34,000	41,634	51,250
West & Southwest N = 11 Range = $28,000 - $115,176	50,162	37,761	43,918	52,000
All Regions N = 57 Range = $22,745 - $122,667	52,101	37,881	44,934	62,992

Four-Year College

	Mean	First Quartile	Median	Third Quartile
North Atlantic N = 19 Range = $37,312 - $84,593	55,358	45,000	54,207	65,000
Great Lakes & Plains N = 19 Range = $22,088 - $70,977	39,953	29,759	37,000	48,104
Southeast N = 14 Range = $32,000 - $77,728	46,235	35,924	42,326	54,800
West & Southwest N = 20 Range = $30,500 - $70,000	47,011	39,852	46,051	51,686
All Regions N = 72 Range = $22,088 - $84,593	47,200	37,078	45,513	55,293

Source: ALA Survey of Librarian Salaries, 2003

Deputy/Associate/Assistant Directors (Page 3 of 3)

Persons who report to the Director and manage major aspects of the library operation. (e.g., technical services, public services, collection development, systems/automation)

University

	Mean	First Quartile	Median	Third Quartile
North Atlantic N = 70 Range = $30,652 - $164,880	77,124	59,128	72,980	88,250
Great Lakes & Plains N = 97 Range = $35,000 - $131,859	75,745	62,835	74,124	88,262
Southeast N = 71 Range = $30,123 - $100,100	66,358	50,072	66,327	82,346
West & Southwest N = 87 Range = $42,840 - $145,000	72,019	58,951	69,377	80,000
All Regions N = 325 Range = $30,123 - $164,880	72,994	58,725	71,184	84,473

All Academic and Public Libraries

	Mean	First Quartile	Median	Third Quartile
North Atlantic N = 302 Range = $24,500 - $164,880	70,417	52,227	67,619	82,074
Great Lakes & Plains N = 353 Range = $22,088 - $131,859	64,485	48,979	63,000	77,140
Southeast N = 276 Range = $22,000 - $110,885	58,268	41,536	56,310	73,781
West & Southwest N = 310 Range = $28,000 - $145,000	68,964	51,938	67,224	83,130
All Regions N = 1,241 Range = $22,000 - $164,880	65,665	49,000	64,191	79,549

Source: ALA Survey of Librarian Salaries, 2003

DEPARTMENT HEADS/COORDINATORS/SENIOR MANAGERS

Persons who supervise one or more professional librarians.

Medium-sized Public Library
(Serving a population of from 25,000 to 99,999)

	Mean	First Quartile	Median	Third Quartile
North Atlantic N = 186 Range = $31,010 - $87,825	55,022	44,514	52,901	63,610
Great Lakes & Plains N = 133 Range = $29,500 - $69,085	47,998	41,772	47,500	53,572
Southeast N = 28 Range = $27,054 - $73,441	41,520	32,197	37,007	47,714
West & Southwest N = 69 Range = $31,851 - $138,338	58,196	49,813	55,902	66,048
All Regions N = 416 Range = $27,054 - $138,338	52,394	42,646	51,050	60,270

Large Public Library
(Serving a population of 100,000 or more)

	Mean	First Quartile	Median	Third Quartile
North Atlantic N = 956 Range = $31,904 - $99,097	55,234	46,862	52,732	61,781
Great Lakes & Plains N = 614 Range = $31,811 - $92,730	55,789	47,947	54,090	62,864
Southeast N = 770 Range = $30,179 - $95,760	52,434	42,615	51,567	59,791
West & Southwest N = 969 Range = $33,840 - $104,568	60,887	50,800	59,712	68,848
All Regions N = 3,309 Range = $30,179 - $104,568	56,341	47,286	55,141	63,543

Source: ALA Survey of Librarian Salaries, 2003

Department Heads/Coordinators/Senior Managers (Page 2 of 3)

Persons who supervise one or more professional librarians.

Two-Year College

	Mean	First Quartile	Median	Third Quartile
North Atlantic N = 17 Range = $37,000 - $83,000	54,342	43,500	52,000	64,000
Great Lakes & Plains N = 9 Range = $38,000 - $94,152	56,027	45,950	55,219	59,077
Southeast N = 11 Range = $36,949 - $83,694	60,715	40,755	61,011	73,822
West & Southwest N = 10 Range = $31,421 - $114,667	65,949	52,071	59,000	79,250
All Regions N = 47 Range = $31,421 - $114,667	58,626	46,422	55,219	69,458

Four-Year College

	Mean	First Quartile	Median	Third Quartile
North Atlantic N = 10 Range = $29,500 - $69,316	49,019	34,750	51,950	60,525
Great Lakes & Plains N = 14 Range = $23,500 - $68,174	47,818	39,799	51,906	53,864
Southeast N = 6 Range = $37,095 - $47,463	41,065	37,484	40,033	44,980
West & Southwest N = 10 Range = $39,000 - $55,000	48,327	42,480	49,315	53,699
All Regions N = 40 Range = $23,500 - $69,316	47,233	39,831	48,878	53,736

Source: ALA Survey of Librarian Salaries, 2003

Department Heads/Coordinators/Senior Managers (Page 3 of 3)

Persons who supervise one or more professional librarians.

University

	Mean	First Quartile	Median	Third Quartile
North Atlantic N = 49 Range = $40,000 - $80,963	57,237	47,094	57,850	66,640
Great Lakes & Plains N = 102 Range = $32,605 - $97,231	57,897	48,817	56,208	64,029
Southeast N = 66 Range = $33,700 - $67,855	52,319	46,320	53,188	58,592
West & Southwest N = 74 Range = $32,500 - $94,584	54,974	43,890	49,620	62,652
All Regions N = 291 Range = $32,500 - $97,231	55,777	46,128	54,600	62,031

All Academic and Public Libraries

	Mean	First Quartile	Median	Third Quartile
North Atlantic N = 1,218 Range = $29,500 - $99,097	55,219	46,416	52,820	61,807
Great Lakes & Plains N = 872 Range = $23,500 - $97,231	54,722	46,873	53,125	61,131
Southeast N = 881 Range = $27,054 - $95,760	52,105	42,346	51,323	59,456
West & Southwest N = 1,132 Range = $31,421 - $138,338	60,270	49,899	59,136	68,761
All Regions N = 4,103 Range = $23,500 - $138,338	55,838	46,680	54,334	63,109

MANAGERS/SUPERVISORS OF SUPPORT STAFF

Persons who supervise support staff in any part of the library but do not supervise professional librarians.

Medium-sized Public Library
(Serving a population of from 25,000 to 99,999)

	Mean	First Quartile	Median	Third Quartile
North Atlantic N = 126 Range = $21,900 - $72,982	45,307	37,492	45,826	51,494
Great Lakes & Plains N = 138 Range = $18,750 - $60,000	37,976	31,537	38,147	43,043
Southeast N = 58 Range = $22,000 - $48,369	34,859	31,228	33,453	39,414
West & Southwest N = 70 Range = $25,400 - $67,366	45,944	39,277	45,263	52,411
All Regions N = 392 Range = $18,750 - $72,982	41,294	34,032	40,694	47,904

Large Public Library
(Serving a population of 100,000 or more)

	Mean	First Quartile	Median	Third Quartile
North Atlantic N = 375 Range = $26,000 - $85,696	45,905	37,615	43,946	52,802
Great Lakes & Plains N = 353 Range = $24,733 - $77,887	46,275	39,204	44,970	51,668
Southeast N = 339 Range = $23,933 - $95,760	45,773	37,527	42,636	53,914
West & Southwest N = 496 Range = $24,864 - $100,698	48,430	40,644	47,228	53,258
All Regions N = 1,563 Range = $23,933 - $100,698	46,761	38,741	45,071	53,054

Source: ALA Survey of Librarian Salaries, 2003

Managers/Supervisors of support staff (Page 2 of 3)

Persons who supervise support staff in any part of the library but do not supervise professional librarians.

Two-Year College

	Mean	First Quartile	Median	Third Quartile
North Atlantic N = 21 Range = $35,680 - $84,400	50,035	43,235	48,000	57,037
Great Lakes & Plains N = 15 Range = $28,000 - $94,889	54,503	34,825	50,231	70,397
Southeast N = 18 Range = $25,522 - $60,535	41,151	36,000	38,158	47,987
West & Southwest N = 28 Range = $22,769 - $79,757	48,929	38,805	46,098	57,757
All Regions N = 82 Range = $22,769 - $94,889	48,525	37,500	44,952	55,267

Four-Year College

	Mean	First Quartile	Median	Third Quartile
North Atlantic N = 39 Range = $24,500 - $64,690	42,772	33,396	40,300	52,705
Great Lakes & Plains N = 32 Range = $27,000 - $66,631	42,469	33,100	38,414	52,040
Southeast N = 23 Range = $35,000 - $67,895	50,174	42,000	50,000	61,213
West & Southwest N = 37 Range = $24,607 - $66,591	41,306	35,308	39,829	46,321
All Regions N = 131 Range = $24,500 - $67,895	43,584	35,088	42,300	51,868

Source: ALA Survey of Librarian Salaries, 2003

Managers/Supervisors of support staff (Page 3 of 3)

Persons who supervise support staff in any part of the library but do not supervise professional librarians.

University

	Mean	First Quartile	Median	Third Quartile
North Atlantic N = 75 Range = $33,280 - $79,136	51,031	42,000	50,772	57,750
Great Lakes & Plains N = 117 Range = $32,000 - $105,125	51,529	40,958	46,667	62,088
Southeast N = 110 Range = $29,690 - $71,581	46,667	40,037	45,701	52,831
West & Southwest N = 123 Range = $25,410 - $96,600	48,477	37,822	44,808	56,722
All Regions N = 425 Range = $25,410 - $105,125	49,300	40,176	46,739	56,166

All Academic and Public Libraries

	Mean	First Quartile	Median	Third Quartile
North Atlantic N = 636 Range = $21,900 - $85,696	46,336	38,036	44,876	53,163
Great Lakes & Plains N = 655 Range = $18,750 - $105,125	45,467	37,642	43,618	51,096
Southeast N = 548 Range = $22,000 - $95,760	44,830	36,606	42,598	51,626
West & Southwest N = 754 Range = $22,769 - $100,698	47,876	40,350	46,109	53,303
All Regions N = 2,593 Range = $18,750 - $105,125	46,246	38,052	44,345	53,054

Source: ALA Survey of Librarian Salaries, 2003

LIBRARIANS WHO DO NOT SUPERVISE
(Page 1 of 3)

Full-time staff with master's degrees from programs in library and information studies accredited by ALA who were not reported earlier and who do not supervise.

Medium-sized Public Library
(Serving a population of from 25,000 to 99,999)

	Mean	First Quartile	Median	Third Quartile
North Atlantic N = 191 Range = $24,000 - $79,586	43,312	38,178	41,646	47,069
Great Lakes & Plains N = 221 Range = $19,037 - $64,308	38,824	34,531	38,429	41,922
Southeast N = 32 Range = $23,000 - $42,217	32,913	30,019	32,274	36,231
West & Southwest N = 122 Range = $23,800 - $64,704	44,243	37,765	43,662	50,921
All Regions N = 566 Range = $19,037 - $79,586	41,172	35,800	40,185	45,302

Large Public Library
(Serving a population of 100,000 or more)

	Mean	First Quartile	Median	Third Quartile
North Atlantic N = 1,217 Range = $27,672 - $72,877	41,653	36,834	40,236	45,307
Great Lakes & Plains N = 921 Range = $23,140 - $75,024	43,585	37,820	42,848	48,384
Southeast N = 749 Range = $22,879 - $71,172	39,328	34,418	36,867	42,745
West & Southwest N = 1,609 Range = $22,450 - $77,358	49,680	41,304	50,254	56,410
All Regions N = 4,496 Range = $22,450 - $77,358	44,534	36,834	42,678	50,612

Source: ALA Survey of Librarian Salaries, 2003

Librarians who do not supervise (Page 2 of 3)

Full-time staff with master's degrees from programs in library and information studies accredited by ALA who were not reported earlier and who do not supervise.

Two-Year College

	Mean	First Quartile	Median	Third Quartile
North Atlantic N = 45 Range = $27,257 - $105,572	56,994	39,833	55,000	66,839
Great Lakes & Plains N = 32 Range = $30,000 - $123,333	59,024	43,360	53,256	69,039
Southeast N = 24 Range = $28,250 - $86,916	45,524	36,000	39,888	54,939
West & Southwest N = 33 Range = $18,500 - $95,851	53,027	39,091	53,000	65,024
All Regions N = 134 Range = $18,500 - $123,333	54,447	38,667	50,000	65,259

Four-Year College

	Mean	First Quartile	Median	Third Quartile
North Atlantic N = 27 Range = $26,900 - $86,190	45,635	37,000	42,000	49,121
Great Lakes & Plains N = 40 Range = $23,400 - $65,489	41,697	35,206	39,459	46,387
Southeast N = 34 Range = $28,000 - $61,544	38,832	33,833	37,790	43,000
West & Southwest N = 36 Range = $27,518 - $73,629	42,812	36,776	39,927	46,455
All Regions N = 137 Range = $23,400 - $86,190	42,055	35,583	40,273	46,085

Source: ALA Survey of Librarian Salaries, 2003

Librarians who do not supervise (Page 3 of 3)

Full-time staff with master's degrees from programs in library and information studies accredited by ALA who were not reported earlier and who do not supervise.

University

	Mean	First Quartile	Median	Third Quartile
North Atlantic N = 303 Range = $27,516 - $99,138	52,102	43,683	50,337	60,000
Great Lakes & Plains N = 478 Range = $29,617 - $108,856	48,758	40,759	46,140	54,319
Southeast N = 328 Range = $25,863 - $82,410	43,424	37,384	41,971	48,373
West & Southwest N = 318 Range = $24,642 - $98,251	49,363	37,043	45,905	55,041
All Regions N = 1,427 Range = $24,642 - $108,856	48,377	39,300	45,876	54,309

All Academic and Public Libraries

	Mean	First Quartile	Median	Third Quartile
North Atlantic N = 1,783 Range = $24,000 - $105,572	44,054	36,841	42,000	48,322
Great Lakes & Plains N = 1,692 Range = $19,037 - $123,333	44,672	37,428	42,855	49,126
Southeast N = 1,167 Range = $22,879 - $86,916	40,416	34,841	38,352	44,419
West & Southwest N = 2,118 Range = $18,500 - $98,251	49,254	40,160	49,212	56,194
All Regions N = 6,760 Range = $18,500 - $123,333	45,210	37,000	42,854	50,841

Source: ALA Survey of Librarian Salaries, 2003

BEGINNING LIBRARIANS

(Page 1 of 3)

Full-time staff with master's degrees from programs in library and information studies accredited by ALA but no professional experience after receiving the degree.

Medium-sized Public Library
(Serving a population of from 25,000 to 99,999)

	Mean	First Quartile	Median	Third Quartile
North Atlantic N = 13 Range = $32,495 - $42,758	37,524	35,000	38,146	38,893
Great Lakes & Plains N = 5 Range = $31,240 - $36,400	33,697	31,332	34,000	35,911
Southeast N = 5 Range = $23,289 - $40,000	28,858	24,145	28,000	34,001
West & Southwest N = 7 Range = $28,968 - $46,104	39,336	33,840	42,048	45,032
All Regions N = 30 Range = $23,289 - $46,104	35,865	32,227	35,911	39,165

Large Public Library
(Serving a population of 100,000 or more)

	Mean	First Quartile	Median	Third Quartile
North Atlantic N = 40 Range = $28,094 - $40,968	34,501	33,850	33,850	35,000
Great Lakes & Plains N = 37 Range = $30,930 - $50,796	36,769	33,766	35,141	39,936
Southeast N = 45 Range = $29,516 - $37,076	33,153	32,389	32,769	34,680
West & Southwest N = 47 Range = $28,745 - $53,508	38,725	36,559	40,546	40,546
All Regions N = 169 Range = $28,094 - $53,508	35,813	33,605	34,680	38,889

Source: ALA Survey of Librarian Salaries, 2003

Beginning Librarians (Page 2 of 3)

Full-time staff with master's degrees from programs in library and information studies accredited by ALA but no professional experience after receiving the degree.

Two-Year College

	Mean	First Quartile	Median	Third Quartile
North Atlantic N = 3 Range = $33,000 - $36,500	34,500		34,00	
Great Lakes & Plains N = 1 Range = $47,533 - $47,533	47,533	47,533	47,533	47.533
Southeast N = 1 Range = $40,000 - $40,000	40,000	40,000	40,000	40,000
West & Southwest N = 3 Range = $38,000 - $50,631	44,877		46,000	
All Regions N = 8 Range = $33,000 - $50,631	40,708	34,625	39,000	47,150

Four-Year College

	Mean	First Quartile	Median	Third Quartile
North Atlantic N = 5 Range = $31,000 - $45,818	38,564	31,000	41,000	44,909
Great Lakes & Plains N = 4 Range = $24,960 - $37,000	29,808	25,538	28,637	35,250
Southeast N = 6 Range = $28,250 - $45,000	35,458	31,438	34,000	40,500
West & Southwest N = 6 Range = $25,936 - $37,333	33,712	31,234	35,000	36,333
All Regions N = 21 Range = $24,960 - $45,818	34,622	30,500	34,000	38,167

Source: ALA Survey of Librarian Salaries, 2003

Beginning Librarians

Full-time staff with master's degrees from programs in library and information studies accredited by ALA but no professional experience after receiving the degree.

University

	Mean	First Quartile	Median	Third Quartile
North Atlantic N = 11 Range = $32,000 - $54,080	41,065	37,000	40,000	47,420
Great Lakes & Plains N = 35 Range = $30,750 - $54,348	37,282	34,299	36,000	39,000
Southeast N = 27 Range = $26,500 - $44,400	35,609	34,000	35,000	38,000
West & Southwest N = 17 Range = $29,000 - $50,100	35,993	30,750	34,000	39,286
All Regions N = 90 Range = $26,500 - $54,348	36,999	33,606	35,938	39,000

All Academic and Public Libraries

	Mean	First Quartile	Median	Third Quartile
North Atlantic N = 72 Range = $28,094 - $54,080	36,332	33,850	34,673	38,817
Great Lakes & Plains N = 82 Range = $24,960 - $54,348	36,592	33,766	35,577	39,165
Southeast N = 84 Range = $23,289 - $45,000	33,933	32,389	34,000	35,000
West & Southwest N = 80 Range = $25,936 - $53,508	38,053	34,002	38,438	40,546
All Regions N = 318 Range = $23,289 - $54,348	36,198	33,350	35,000	39,000

Source: ALA Survey of Librarian Salaries, 2003

Discussion

Summary of Results

People interested in a particular type of library or a particular type of work, or a particular region will have their own way of drawing conclusions from the results of this survey. However, the results may be summarized in a very general way by noting that this survey included 15,856 salaries ranging from $18,500 to $276,500 with a mean of $51,362 and a median of $47,914. Another way to summarize is to look at mean salaries paid to particular types of positions, mean salaries paid by particular types of libraries, or mean salaries paid in particular parts of the U.S.

Salaries by Type of Position

The six positions are shown in rank order by mean of salaries paid on Table 1. Also shown is the mean of salaries paid in 2002, the dollar difference and the percent increase.

Table 1. Rank Order of Position Types by Mean of Salaries Paid

Title	2003 Salary	2002 Salary	Change Amount	Percent
Director	79,385	75,714	+3,691	4.9
Deputy/Associate/Assistant Directors	65,665	62,847	+2,818	4.5
Department Heads/Coordinators/Senior Managers	55,838	54,260	+1,578	2.9
Managers/Supervisors of Support Staff	46,246	44,549	+1,697	3.8
Librarians who do not supervise	45,210	44,279	+931	2.1
Beginning Librarians	36,198	35,051	+1,147	3.3

SOURCE: ALA SURVEY OF LIBRARIAN SALARIES, 2003

The percentage of increase in the means of this year's 15,856 salaries over the means of last year's 14,805 salaries is 3.6 percent. This figure is 0.7% higher than the increase in salaries for all "civilian workers" for the same time period as reported by the U.S. Bureau of Labor Statistics in their Employment Cost Index. The percent change from March 02 to March 03 for civilian workers was 2.9%. The increase for the state and local government subset of civilian workers was 3.1%. Data on the Employment Cost Index is published in each issue of the *Monthly Labor Review*, but those figures are now several months behind what can be found on the Web. Percent change figures used in this paragraph were found on July 18, 2003 at: http://www.bls.gov/news.release/pdf/eci.pdf.

Salaries by Type of Library

For all six categories, salaries were usually highest in university or two-year college libraries and lowest in medium-sized public libraries.

Salaries by Region of the U.S.

In order to determine which region has the highest salaries, we analyzed the six positions and the five library size/type categories. When the region with the highest mean salary was marked for each position in each size/type category, North

Atlantic was checked 37 percent of the time and West and Southwest was highest 43 percent of the time. Great Lakes and Plains was highest five times. Southeast was never highest. This pattern is similar to last year, except that in 2003 West and Southwest was the highest more often and North Atlantic was highest less often. The lowest mean salary was in the Southeast 77 percent of the time. Great Lakes and Plains was lowest four times, and West and Southwest was lowest once. North Atlantic was lowest twice.

Problem with Categories New in 1999

There is one problem with the above summary paragraphs, stemming from changes made in the questionnaire in 1999. For libraries in the Association of Research Libraries (ARL), we did not have salaries in two categories: Department Heads/Coordinators/Senior Managers and Managers/Supervisors of Support Staff. We use data already collected by ARL for ARL libraries in our sample, and ARL does not use those two categories. Therefore we knew we do not have salaries in those categories for the 19 ARL libraries in our sample this year. The absence may have an impact on the summaries by type of position and by region.

Complicating Factors

When designing this survey in the early 1980s, we were aware that several aspects of the patterns of employment in libraries would complicate our efforts. As we talked with respondents and users of the reports over the years, we gained additional insights into several factors, which should be taken into consideration when using these results.

The Meaning of "Full-Time"

The questionnaire asked about salaries for **full-time** positions only, but full-time was not defined. There are at least two problems in this area: How many months in a year is full-time? How do you report people who work full-time in the library but part-time at one job and part-time at another?

The months in a year problem primarily affects academic libraries where librarians sometimes have academic year contracts for less than twelve months. In this survey, respondents are asked to indicate the number of months a salary covers and the computer calculated twelve months at the same rate. Appendix F shows how often less-than-twelve-month salaries occur.

The Meaning of "Professional"

In the early years of this survey, respondents were asked to report only salaries paid to professionals, but the word "professional" was not defined. Instead, each position was described in such a way that professional responsibility was clearly implied. Instructions told the respondent to list all incumbents in these positions "regardless of academic credentials." We accepted the judgement of the respondent that the salaries reported were for professional work but found out, when we called about low salaries (see below) that some respondents had doubts about whether a particular incumbent could be described as "professional." When such doubts were expressed, we asked the respondent to make a decision based on the definition in ALA's statement on "Library Education and Personnel Utilization." That policy has since been revised and has a new title, Library and Information Studies Education
and Human Resource Utilization". However, the definition relevant here is the same. (See Appendix B, Policy 54.1, Section 8) In 1990, that definition was added to the instructions. Beginning with the 1991 survey, we asked respondents to report only staff *with master's degrees from programs in library and information studies accredited by ALA.*

Salaries Below $22,000

In previous years, this report has described the methodology used to determine the cut-off point below which salaries were investigated as probably not being full-time, professional work. The cut-off point for the 2003 survey was $22,000. Of the 15,878 salaries initially considered usable, 26 were below $22,000 (less than 1%). Staff at the Library Research Center used e-mail or telephone to contact the person named as the respondent at the 21 libraries involved. They learned that 22 salaries were for part-time work, were for non-professional positions, or were filled out in error. Those 22 salaries were dropped from the data file used for this report. The dropped salaries had been reported primarily because the respondent had misunderstood the instructions. Once the salaries were dropped, the total usable number of salaries was

15,856. Four (4) salaries of less than $22,000 did remain in the file. Of these, three were in public libraries and one was in an academic library.

Job Levels or Faculty Ranks

The wording of this questionnaire is based on an assumption that librarians are compensated at a particular amount for assuming a particular level of responsibility. However, in many libraries that is not true. Some libraries use a system of levels in their compensation structure (e.g., Librarian I, II, III, IV) to account for the background a person brings to a job and the amount of experience the person has. Some academic libraries pay salaries based on faculty rank rather than work done. In many academic libraries where librarians have faculty rank and titles, they are compensated as Instructor, Assistant Professor, Associate Professor or Professor and not as any one of the position categories on our questionnaire. We do not attempt to account for this variety within the structure of our questionnaire.

Several respondents and reviewers of this report have recommended in the past that we collect salary data for librarian levels or ranks. We have considered this seriously, but concluded that it would be at least as confusing as the current method due to the fact that levels and ranks mean different things in different libraries.

Level of Experience

Respondents occasionally ask us to ask for and report salaries in a way that takes into account the years of experience that an incumbent possesses. Unfortunately, providing that information would be a burden on respondents and reporting it would make this report overly complex. This report does take such factors into account in two ways: beginning librarians are reported in a separate table and are not included in salary data for other positions; and data for all positions show figures at the first and third quartile as well as the mean, median, and range.

Appendix A

Compensation Surveys Providing Information on Library Workers

Most library salary surveys listed below are conducted on a regular schedule (annual or biennial) and on a regional or national basis. The library literature should be monitored for reports of one-time surveys by individual libraries or associations. Some state library agencies collect salary and benefits data as part of their ongoing statistical gathering efforts from libraries within their own state. There is wide variation, however, in what data are collected and how these are compiled and reported. Most collect only public library data. Academic and school library data may be collected by other state agencies.

In addition, some state library associations collect salary data, issue recommended salary guidelines, set minimum salaries for professional positions, or publish reports in association journals or newsletters. As of August 2003, eighteen states had established recommended minimum salaries. These include: Connecticut, Illinois, Indiana, Iowa, Louisiana, Maine, Massachusetts, New Jersey, North Carolina, Ohio, Pennsylvania, Rhode Island, South Carolina, South Dakota, Texas, Vermont, West Virginia, and Wisconsin. Specific amounts are not listed here because these are updated regularly by the associations. The latest figures can be found in the most recent classified section of *American Libraries* or *College & Research Libraries News*.

A list of state library agency and association addresses can be found in *The Bowker Annual: Library and Book Trade Almanac* or on the Internet at www.dpi.state.wi.us/dpi/dlcl/pld/statelib.html and www.ala.org/ under "Our Organization/Chapters."

Individual libraries will sometimes conduct private surveys of institutions of comparable size or in the same geographical area, either through an outside consulting firm or by calling libraries informally. For the most part, these surveys are not published, although the initiating library will often share results with participating libraries. Some library workers are also conducting surveys that compare their salaries with other professions and occupations within their jurisdiction in an effort to achieve pay equity with positions requiring comparable skills, effort, responsibilities and working conditions.

Academic Libraries

Association of Research Libraries. *ARL Annual Salary Survey*. Washington, D.C.: ARL, 1973-.

> The 2002-03 compilation consists of detailed tables of salaries for over 12,000 professional positions based on data collected from ARL member libraries and analyzed by job category, years of experience, sex, minority status, size of library, and geographic region. Included in the publication are tables for medical, law, Canadian libraries and non-university research libraries. Information on this survey can be found at www.arl.org/stats/salary/index.html.
>
> To order, contact ARL Publications Distribution Center, PO Box 531, Annapolis Junction, MD 20701-0531, 301/362-8196, (fax) 301/206-9789, (e-mail) pubs@arl.org.

College and University Professional Association for Human Resources. 2002-03 *Administrative Compensation Survey*. Washington, D.C.: CUPA-HR.

The survey includes data on college and university administrative positions from 1,415 public and private institutions. The tables in the survey present the median salary according to institutional budget, enrollment, and classification. Directors of library services are included.

The survey is available from CUPA-HR, 1233 20th St., NW, Suite 301, Washington, D.C. 20035-1250, 202/429-0311, (fax) 202/429-0149, (web) www.cupahr.org.

College and University Professional Association for Human Resources. 2002-03 *Mid-Level Administrative/Professional Salary Survey*. Washington, D.C.: CUPA-HR.

This survey features median salary data from 1,131 public and private institutions on 135 positions, including reference specialist, cataloging specialist, Webmaster and other technology based positions. Data are organized by operating budget size and include regional comparisons. See contact information above.

Public Libraries

American Library Association. Public Library Association. *Public Library Data Service Statistical Report 2003*. Chicago, IL: PLA.

The current edition is designed to aid in and enhance the public library planning and evaluation process and help library managers identify top performing libraries, compare service levels and technology usage, and provide documentation for funding requests. Also included are the results of a special survey on children's services. Order from ALA Order Fulfillment, PO Box 932501, Atlanta, GA 31193-2501, 866/746-7252, for $80 with discounts for PLA and ALA members (ISBN 0-8389-8223-9).

Evelina R. Moulder. "Salaries of Municipal Officials, 2003" in *The Municipal Year Book,* 2003. Washington, D.C.: International City/County Management Association.

Chief librarian salaries for local public libraries are included with earnings of other city department heads. These are reported by geographic region, population size, city type (i.e., central, suburban, independent) and form of government. *The Municipal Year Book* is published in April of each year and includes salary data from the previous year. To order, call 800-745-8780, (web) http://bookstore.icma.org/.

Sandstedt, Carl R. *Salary Survey: West-North-Central States.* St. Peters, Mo.: St. Charles City-County Library.

This annual survey provides data for directors, assistant directors, department heads, starting MLS, and several support positions for public libraries in West-North-Central States (North Dakota, South Dakota, Nebraska, Kansas, Minnesota, Iowa, Missouri). Average salaries are presented by size of library budget. Also includes per FTE costs, per capita support, and per capita materials budget.

St. Charles City-County Library District, 425 Spencer Rd., Box 529, St. Peters, MO 63376. Available online at www.win.org/library/.

School Libraries

Educational Research Service. *Salaries and Wages for Professional and Support Personnel in Public Schools*, Arlington, VA: ERS, 2002-03.

ERS publishes an annual report of salaries for public school personnel, which includes data for school librarians and library clerks. The report covers scheduled salaries for professional personnel and actual salaries paid for professional and support personnel by enrollment group, per pupil expenditure, and geographic region. It also includes year-to-year, five-year, and ten-year information on trends in public school salaries and wages, with comparisons to the Consumer Price Index for each of these periods. Available from ERS, 2000 Clarendon Blvd., Arlington, VA 22201, 703/248-6244, (fax) 703/243-8410.

"Expenditures for Resources in School Library Media Centers." *School Library Journal*.

As part of a report every two years on budgets for and expenditures by school library media centers, some median and mean salary data for media specialists are reported by level of school. Included are comparisons of schools with and without district level library media coordinators. *School Library Journal*, 360 Park Avenue South, NY, NY 10010, 646-746-6759, (fax) 646-746-6689, (e-mail) slj@reedbusiness.com.

Specialized Libraries

American Association of Law Libraries. *Biennial Salary Survey and Organizational Characteristics 2003*. Chicago, IL: AALL.

The report summarizes salary information for law libraries with three following sections that cover academic libraries, private firm/corporate libraries and state, court and county libraries. The data is broken out and crossed-tabbed by position, region, gender, education, years in current position and years of library experience and further by geographical regions in the U.S.

Contact AALL, 53 W. Jackson Blvd., Suite 940, Chicago, IL 60604, 312/939-4764 x12, (fax) 312/431-1097, (web) www.aallnet.org. AALL members may browse the online edition free of charge.

Association of Academic Health Sciences Libraries. *Annual Statistics of Medical School Libraries in the United States and Canada*. Seattle, WA: AAHSLD.

Salaries are provided for director, associate director, division head, department head, other librarians, and entry level positions. Minimum, maximum and mean are provided for the positions and arranged by region.

It's available at no cost to members of AAHSL and $250 for nonmembers. The current edition and previous editions may be ordered by contacting AAHSL, 2150 N. 107th St., #205, Seattle, WA 98133, 206/367-8704, (fax) 206/367-8777, (web) www.aahsl.org.

Medical Library Association. *Health Sciences Librarian Compensation: Results of MLA's 2001 Salary Survey*. Chicago: MLA, 2001.

More than 1,900 members provided data for the 2001 triennial salary survey, available in summary format to MLA's members via the Association's website, www.mlanet.org. The summary offers detailed information by job title, geographical area, type of institution, and more. Contact Kate Corcoran, MLA, 65 E. Wacker Pl., Suite 1900, Chicago, IL 60601-7298, 312/419-9094, ext. 12.

Special Libraries Association. *SLA Annual Salary Survey*. Washington, D.C.: SLA, 2002.

Salaries are reported at the 10th, 25th, 50th (median), 75th and 90th percentiles and contain breakdowns by industry, geographic region, administrative responsibility, sex, education level, and experience. Data for the U.S. and Canada are presented in separate tables.

The Salary Survey is a comprehensive report containing the most accurate U.S. and Canadian salary information gathered by a member survey. A wide variety of variables are covered including industry type, geographical area, job title, budget range and years of experience.

The report is available to SLA members for $45, $125 non-members. Contact Special Libraries Association, 1700 18th St., N.W., Washington, D.C. 20009-2514, 202/939-3681, (fax) 202/265-9317.

Other

Association for Library and Information Science Education. *ALISE Statistical Report and Database*. Reston, VA: ALISE, 1980-.

Average and median salaries for faculty and administrators in ALISE member schools are provided in this annual report by sex, rank and term of appointment.

Back issues (1981-) of the report are available from ALISE, 1009 Commerce Park Dr., #150, PO Box 4219, Oak Ridge, TN 37831-4219, 865/481-0155, (fax) 865/481-0390, (web) www.alise.org/publications/. This annual report is published in the summer.

College and University Professional Association for Human Resources. 2002-03 *National Faculty Salary Survey by Discipline and Rank in Private Two- and Four-Year Colleges and Universities*. Washington, D.C.: CUPA-HR.

College and University Professional Association for Human Resources. 2002-03 *National Faculty Salary Survey by Discipline and Rank in Public Two- and Four-Year Colleges and Universities*. Washington, D.C.: CUPA-HR.

Annual surveys collect data for five faculty ranks in 80 disciplines and major fields. Communications, Communication Technologies, Computer Information Sciences, and Library Sciences are included. The listings are for those who teach in library science programs, not those who hold faculty rank as academic librarians. Contact CUPA-HR, 1233 20th St., NW, Suite 301, Washington, D.C. 20036-1250, 202/429-0311, (fax) 202/429-0149, (web) www.cupahr.org.

"Placements and Salaries 2002." *Library Journal*.

> An annual survey since 1951 of ALA-accredited library and information studies education programs (usually published in the October 15th issue of *Library Journal* with data from previous calendar year.) For each reporting school, the low, high, average and median salaries are reported for men, women, and total placements. This information is also provided for five regions of the U.S. An additional table shows the distribution of high, low, average and median salaries by type of library for men, women and total placements.

Employee Benefits

Although some states collect data on employee benefits, little information is collected on a regional or national level on a regular basis for library workers.

PROVIDENCE Associates, Inc. *Public Library Work Benefits Survey*. Denton, TX.

> Results of a survey of 25 public libraries in 1997 provides salary ranges and average salaries for 5 staff levels, plus data on vacation days, sick leave, leave of absence, pension plans, health and life insurance, and other benefits. Single copies from PROVIDENCE Associates, Inc., 488 Mill Dr., 2nd floor, Cottonwood, AZ 86326-5340, (e-mail) aneyeforit@sedona.net. Look for the next survey in 2003.

Salary Surveys for Other Library Workers and Related Information Professionals

For salary data on other types of workers that may be employed in libraries, the following surveys might be useful:

Abbott, Langer and Associates, Inc., Dept NET, 548 First St., Crete, IL 60417, 708/672-4200, (fax) 708/672-4674, (web) www.abbott-langer.com. Conducts annual or biennial salary surveys for the following fields: legal and related jobs in business and industry; industrial engineers; plant and facilities managers and engineers; consulting engineering firms; consulting firms; independent lab/testing/inspection firms; geologists; human resources/personnel department; service department; nonprofit organizations; research and development; manufacturing; food and beverage processing; security/loss prevention dept.; MIS/data processing; accounting departments; accounting firms; advertising agencies; sales/marketing management; direct marketing; life sciences and telecommunications.

> *Compensation in Nonprofit Organizations* contains information on salaries of Directors of Information with this type of employer. Mean, median, first and third quartile, and first and ninth decile data, salary ranges, current salaries, and total compensation (salaries plus bonuses) are reported by supervisory responsibility, type of nonprofit organization, total annual budget, geographic scope of organization, number of employees, region, state, and metropolitan area, and type of organization vs. remaining variables.

> *Available Pay Survey Reports: An Annotated Bibliography* (4th ed.) by Dr. Steven Langer (2002) contains annotations of over 1,200 pay survey reports, both domestic and foreign. Annotations are indexed by source, geographic area, type of employer, and job title/function/college curricula.

The *Library Mosaics*, a bi-monthly magazine for support staff in libraries, media and information centers has published the "2003 Salary Survey" by Raymond Roney and Charlie Fox in the July/August issue. It provides a general overview of support staff salaries, salary ceilings and pay equity. *Library Mosaics*, PO Box 5171, Culver City, CA 90231, 310/645-4998, (e-mail) editor@librarymosaics.com.

AMS Foundation Business Survey Group. The AMSF Salary Report provides salary information on over 140 occupations and 15,000 employees from 667 participating offices/plants/stores. The report, which includes pay data on a national, regional, and metropolitan basis, 14 industries, number of employees and fiscal size, points out how incomes vary by geographical area. Order through AMS Foundation, Dept. NET, 548 First St., Crete, IL, 60417, 708/672-4200, (fax) 708/672-4674.

U.S. Department of Labor, Bureau of Labor Statistics, National Compensation Survey program produces information on wages by occupation for many metropolitan areas and also for the nation as a whole. It provides data on occupational earnings, employer costs for wages, salaries, and benefits, and details of employer-provided benefit and establishment practices. This umbrella program combines the Occupational Compensation Surveys, the Employment Cost Index, and the Employee Benefits Survey and is published annually. For more information, phone 202/691-6199, or visit URL http://stats.bls.gov/ncs/.

Appendix B

ALA Policies Relating to Salary Issues

The following are policies endorsed by the ALA Council and included in the "ALA Policy Manual" which appears annually in the *ALA Handbook of Organization*.

Policy #54.1 Library and Information Studies Education and Human Resource Utilization

8. The title "Librarian" carries with it the connotation of "professional" in the sense that professional tasks are those which require a special background and education on the basis of which library needs are identified, problems are analyzed, goals are set, and original and creative solutions are formulated for them, integrating theory into practice, and planning, organizing, communicating, and administering successful programs of service to users of the library's materials and services. In defining services to users, the professional person recognizes potential users as well as current ones, and designs services, which will reach all who could benefit from them.

9. The title "Librarian" therefore should be used only to designate positions in libraries, which utilize the qualifications and impose the responsibilities suggested above. Positions which are primarily devoted to the routine application of established rules and techniques, however useful and essential to the effective operation of a library's ongoing services, should not carry the word "Librarian" in the job title.

11. The salaries for each category should offer a range of promotional steps sufficient to permit a career-in-rank. The top salary in any category should overlap the beginning salary in the next higher category, in order to give recognition to the value of experience and knowledge gained on the job.

18. The first professional category—Librarian or Specialist—assumes responsibilities that are professional in the sense described in paragraph #8 above. A well-rounded liberal education plus graduate-level study in the field of specialization (either in librarianship or in a relevant field) are seen as the minimum preparation for the kinds of assignments implied. The title, however, is given for a position entailing professional responsibilities and not automatically upon achievement of the academic degree.

19. The Senior categories assume relevant professional experience as well as qualifications beyond those required for admission to the first professional ranks. Normally, it is assumed that such advanced qualification shall be held in some specialty, either in a particular aspect of librarianship or some relevant subject field. Subject specializations are as applicable in the Senior Librarian category as they are in the Senior Specialist category.

20. Administrative responsibilities entail high-level specialty, and appointment to positions in top administration should normally require the qualifications of Senior Librarian with a specialization in administration. This category, however, is not limited to administrators, whose specialty is only one of several specializations of value to the library service. There are many areas of special

knowledge within librarianship which are equally important and to which equal recognition in prestige and salary should be given. Highly qualified persons with specialist responsibilities in some aspects of librarianship—archives, bibliography, reference, for example—should be eligible for advanced status and financial rewards without being forced to abandon for administrative responsibilities their areas of major competence.

Policy #54.4 Comparable Rewards

The American Library Association supports salary administration, which gives reasonable and comparable recognition to positions having administrative, technical, subject, and linguistic requirements. It is recognized that all such specialist competencies can be intellectually vigorous and meet demanding professional operational needs. In administering such a policy, it can be a useful guide that, in major libraries, as many non-administrative specialties be assigned to the top classifications, as are administrative staff. Whenever possible there should be as many at the top rank with less than 30 percent administrative load as there are at the highest rank carrying over 70 percent administrative load.

Policy #54.7 Security of Employment for Library Employees

Security of employment, as an elementary right, guarantees specifically.....a sufficient degree of economic security to make employment in the library attractive to men and women of ability.

Policy #54.8 The Library's Pay Plan

Libraries should have a well constructed and well-administered pay plan based on systematic analysis and evaluation of jobs in the library and which will assure equal pay for equal work. (Note: For text of full statement, see the end of this section.)

Policy #54.9 Permanent Part-Time Employment

The right to earn a living includes a right to part-time employment on a par with full-time employment, including prorated pay and fringe benefits, opportunity for advancement and protection of tenure, access to middle and upper level jobs, and exercise of full responsibilities at any level.

ALA shall create more voluntarily chosen upgraded permanent part-time jobs in its own organization and supports similar action on the part of all libraries.

Policy #54.10 Equal Opportunity and Salaries

The American Library Association supports and works for the achievement of equal salaries and opportunity for employment and promotion for men and women.

The Association fully supports the concept of comparable wages for comparable work that aims at levels of pay for female-oriented occupations equal to those of male-oriented occupations; ALA therefore supports all legal and legislative efforts to achieve wages for library workers commensurate with wages in other occupations with similar qualifications, training, and responsibilities.

ALA particularly supports the efforts of those library workers who have documented, and are legally challenging, the practice of discriminatory salaries, and whose success will benefit all library workers throughout the nation.

Policy #54.11 Collective Bargaining

The American Library Association recognizes the principle of collective bargaining as one of the methods of conducting labor-management relations used by private and public institutions. The Association affirms the right of eligible library employees to organize and bargain collectively with their employers, or to refrain from organizing and bargaining collectively, without fear of reprisal.

Policy #54.18 Advertising Salary Ranges

Available ranges shall be given for positions listed in any placement services provided by ALA and its units. A regional salary guide delineating the latest minimum salary figures recommended by state library associations shall be made available from any placement services provided by ALA and its units. All ALA and unit publications printing classified job advertisements shall include a regional salary guide delineating the latest minimum salary figures recommended by state library association for library positions.

Full Text of Policy # 54.8: The Library's Pay Plan*

The American Library Association believes that an important factor in establishing and maintaining good library service is adequate pay for library employees as exemplified in a well-constructed and well-administered pay plan. A knowledge of the principles on which sound salary administration is based must be the foundation of an equitable pay plan. To aid the library's governing board, its administration, and its staff in the formulation, promulgation, and operation of such a pay plan, the ALA Board on Personnel Administration sets forth in a series of related statements the principles of salary planning and administration.

1. A sound pay plan will be predicated on a systematic analysis and evaluation of jobs in the library, and will reflect the current organization and objectives of the library, recognizing different levels of difficulty and responsibility inherent in various positions, whether these are classified as professional, nonprofessional, administrative, specialist, maintenance, or trade; the relationship among positions in terms of difficulty and responsibility will thus be expressed in a unified plan which will integrate all types of service and will assure equal pay for equal work.

2. An equitable salary schedule will be provided for each class of position that is comparable to that received by persons employed in analogous work in the area and required to have analogous training and qualifications.

The salaries of nonprofessional employees, maintenance and skilled trade workers employed by the library system will compare with those of local workers performing similar duties. The salary schedules for professional library positions, in the case of the community where the pay scale does not meet competing rates outside, may need to exceed the prevailing local level for other professional personnel. Since the recruiting of professionally trained librarians is on a nation-wide basis, the library system must compete with rates paid in the country as a whole in order to obtain and retain a high quality of professional personnel. In libraries in educational institutions (elementary, secondary, and higher education) the professional librarians will normally be on the faculty pay plan, with the salary schedules of the various classes of faculty rank adjusted to compensate equitably for such factors as shorter vacations and longer work week; where a separate pay plan is used, it will be comparable with that of the faculty and adjusted to compensate equitably for such factors as vacation and work week.

3. An equitable salary schedule will provide for each class of position a minimum and a maximum salary and a series of increments within each salary range, such increments to be granted on the basis of demonstrated competence, individual development (whether through growth on the job or through formal education), and attitude.

*Note: This policy was passed by the ALA Council in July 1955. It still remains a useful statement regarding the administration of a library's pay plan. Readers should note, however, that the references to the Board on Personnel Administration are not applicable since this unit is no longer in existence

4. The library system in developing a pay plan, and in reviewing it to maintain its adequacy, will identify one or more key positions in the professional and in the other services, set salary schedules for these positions which are comparable to prevailing rates for such positions, and develop and adjust the salary schedule for other levels of positions in relation to the salary schedules set for each of these key positions.

5. The pay plan ladder consisting of the salary schedules for the various classes of positions will provide an orderly progression from the lowest to the highest schedule, with each schedule reflecting properly the difference in level of duties and responsibilities of positions in that classification from those in the schedule below and above it but without wide gaps or serious overlapping between schedules.

6. An equitable pay plan will reflect living costs in the community, the cost of maintaining an appropriate level of living, and the ability of the jurisdiction to pay for the service.

7. All policies and rules concerning the operation and administration of the pay plan will be set forth clearly in writing and will accompany the pay plan.

8. Though final approval and adoption of the pay plan and rules for its operation rest with the governing board and administration of the library, it is desirable that the library staff participates in the formulation of both the plan and its operating rules.

9. Each staff member will be informed of the salary schedule for his or her class of position, of the relation of that schedule to the pay plan as a whole, and of the policies and rules governing the operation of the plan.

The current studies of the ALA Board on Personnel Administration giving salary data for key positions will provide useful material for the library system in developing and maintaining the adequacy of its pay plan.

Appendix C

Technical Considerations

Formation of Library Groups

As in previous years, the survey samples were selected from two library universes – public and academic. The public library universe included all public libraries serving populations of 25,000 or more and was stratified into two classes – those serving populations of from 25,000 to 99,999 and those serving populations of 100,000 or more.

The academic library universe was stratified into three categories: two-year college, four-year college, and university using the 2000 Academic Library Survey file. This file includes codes for the categories created by the Carnegie Foundation for the Advancement of Teaching in 1994. Our "two-year college" corresponds to the Carnegie category "Associate of Arts." Our "four-year college" category corresponds to the Carnegie Categories "Baccalaureate I and II." Our "university" includes the Carnegie categories "Master's I and II, Doctoral I and II, and Research I and II."

Within each of these five strata, libraries were furthered stratified into four geographic areas used frequently by National Center for Education Statistics (NCES): North Atlantic, Great Lakes and Plains, Southeast, West, and Southwest. A list of states included in each region is provided in Table C-1. As in previous surveys, the five library classes and four geographic areas were combined to form twenty groups from which samples were selected. Tables C2-C7 show the size of each group, the size of the sample, and the size of the return.

Sample Selection and Return

The size of the sample for each type/size/geographic strata was determined by using a proportional sampling procedure that took into account the size of the population in each group and the expected return rate for the survey. The public library sample was selected using a file from the NCES containing 2000 data on all public libraries submitted to NCES by state library agencies as part of the Federal State Cooperative System for Public Library Data (FSCS). This file includes data on the number of staff with master's degrees from programs in library and information studies accredited by ALA. Before selecting the sample, LRC dropped from the sampling frame libraries that did not have at least two of such personnel and libraries that had refused to respond in the years from 1990 through 2002 for reasons that seemed unlikely to change.

The procedure for selecting the academic library sample was similar to the procedure followed in previous years. The Library Research Center (LRC) created a sampling frame by using the universe file described above (see second paragraph). This file includes data on the number of staff who are "librarians and other professionals". Before selecting the sample, LRC dropped from the sampling frame libraries that did not have at least two of such personnel and libraries that had refused to respond in the years from 1990 through 2002 for reasons that seemed unlikely to change. Then LRC screened out several sets of institutions. Removed were institutions with fewer than two full-time professionals and institutions categorized as "specialized" by the Carnegie Corporation for the Advancement of Teaching. Those institutions offer degrees ranging from the bachelor's to the doctorate, at least 50 percent of which are in a single specialized field, e.g., "theological seminaries, Bible colleges, and other institutions offering degrees in religion," and "Schools of art, music, and design." Specialized institutions often declined to respond in the early years of this survey. Also excluded were four sets of institutions whose individual members had been unable to respond in the past. In New York, the seventeen institutions that are part of the City University of New York were removed because librarians there have full academic status and salary is not related to position description. Public two-year schools in California were removed for the same reason, as were the fourteen members of the state university system in

Pennsylvania. Also in Pennsylvania, we removed all but the main campus of Pennsylvania State University because librarians at other campuses declined to respond in the past and referred us to the main campus.

In addition to the 901 returns analyzed for this report, we also received 15 returns that could not be used. They fell into the following categories:

- Five were from academic libraries where none of the staff are full-time or none of the full-time staff had master's degrees from programs in library and information studies accredited by ALA.

- Eight were from academic libraries where salary data are confidential by institutional policy or where no one had access to the data.

- Two were returned blank for other reasons.

Procedure

The questionnaire and cover letter were mailed on April 11, 2003. A postage-paid business reply envelope was enclosed to encourage response. A second mailing was sent to all non-respondents in May. A third mailing was sent in June only to non-respondents in several strata where response was under 70 percent. Two aspects of the procedure were new this year. Directors in public libraries serving populations of over 500,000 were sent a special letter that recognized the problems involved in reporting in large staff and invited them to consult with the project director for possible solutions. Also, in previous years the reminder packet had included a copy of the original letter plus a brightly colored reminder notice. In 2003 a special reminder letter was sent. Questionnaires were returned to the Library Research Center (LRC) of the University of Illinois Graduate School of Library and Information Science, where they were coded, entered into a data file, cleaned, and analyzed using SPSS for Windows.

Again this year a special procedure was followed for libraries that are members of the Association of Research Libraries (ARL). ARL, which includes about 100 of the largest university libraries in the U.S., conducts its own annual salary survey. Data are gathered for salaries as of July 1 and published the following spring. ARL libraries are also included in the sample for the ALA survey. In the past, some have declined to answer because they are unable to spend time completing another salary questionnaire. For the 2003 survey, ARL again agreed to cooperate with us to save work for everyone. After the sample was selected, we identified the ARL libraries on the list and sent the directors a special mailing asking them to release salaries already on file with ARL. Nineteen of the twenty-five ARL libraries in the sample agreed to release data. We sent ARL a list of the ARL position codes that matched the position descriptions in our questionnaire and ARL sent salary data to LRC electronically for those positions in the selected institutions. These salaries were entered into the data file along with salaries reported on the questionnaire.

This procedure worked well and saved time both in the libraries involved and in survey processing. It has two drawbacks, however. ARL does not specify that salaries should be reported only for staff with master's degrees from programs in library and information studies accredited by ALA and some ARL libraries include "other professionals" as well as librarians. For the most part, however, we expect that those "other professionals" are in the ARL position code of "Functional Specialist" which was *not* on the list of codes we requested from ARL. Also, the ARL survey does not ask respondents to indicate the type of staff supervised which is the key distinction between two categories in the ALA survey: Department Heads/Coordinators/Senior Managers and Managers/Supervisors of Support Staff. Because we are aware of the burden it will place on ARL libraries to ask them to complete the new questionnaire, we decided to use as much data as we could from ARL and accept the fact that salaries at ARL libraries are not included for the two positions just noted.

Table C-1. States in Four Regions of the U.S.

North Atlantic	Great Lakes and Plains	Southeast	West and Southwest
Connecticut	Illinois	Alabama	Alaska
Delaware	Indiana	Arkansas	Arizona
District of Columbia	Iowa	Florida	California
Maine	Kansas	Georgia	Colorado
Maryland	Michigan	Kentucky	Hawaii
Massachusetts	Minnesota	Louisiana	Idaho
New Hampshire	Missouri	Mississippi	Montana
New Jersey	Nebraska	North Carolina	Nevada
New York	North Dakota	South Carolina	New Mexico
Pennsylvania	Ohio	Tennessee	Oklahoma
Rhode Island	South Dakota	Virginia	Oregon
Vermont	Wisconsin	West Virginia	Texas
			Utah
			Washington
			Wyoming

SOURCE: STATISITCS OF PUBLIC LIBRARIES, 1977-1978 (NCES, 1982)

Table C-2. Medium-Sized Public Libraries: Size of Group, Sample, Return

	GROUP	SAMPLE		RETURN	
	#	#	% of Group	#	% of Sample
North Atlantic	341	124	36.4	83	66.9
Great Lakes and Plains	319	117	36.7	83	70.9
Southeast	191	70	36.6	54	77.1
West and Southwest	189	70	37.0	55	78.6
TOTAL	1,040	381	36.6	275	72.2

Table C-3. Large Public Libraries: Size of Group, Sample, Return

	GROUP	SAMPLE		RETURN	
	#	#	% of Group	#	% of Sample
North Atlantic	62	59	95.2	45	76.3
Great Lakes and Plains	96	57	59.4	49	86.0
Southeast	138	62	44.9	51	82.3
West and Southwest	165	83	50.3	67	80.7
TOTAL	461	261	56.6	212	81.2

Table C-4. Two-Year College Libraries: Size of Group, Sample, Return

	GROUP	SAMPLE		RETURN	
	#	#	% of Group	#	% of Sample
North Atlantic	159	47	29.6	31	66.0
Great Lakes and Plains	165	50	30.3	36	72.0
Southeast	239	70	29.3	38	54.3
West and Southwest	178	54	30.3	30	55.6
TOTAL	741	221	29.8	135	61.1

Table C-5. Four-Year College Libraries: Size of Group, Sample, Return

	GROUP	SAMPLE		RETURN	
	#	#	% of Group	#	% of Sample
North Atlantic	138	46	33.3	28	60.9
Great Lakes and Plains	171	51	29.8	33	64.7
Southeast	151	46	30.5	26	56.5
West and Southwest	70	46	65.7	32	69.6
TOTAL	530	189	35.7	119	63.0

Table C-6. University Libraries: Size of Group, Sample, Return

	GROUP	SAMPLE		RETURN	
	#	#	% of Group	#	% of Sample
North Atlantic	192	58	30.2	39	67.2
Great Lakes and Plains	172	52	30.2	43	82.7
Southeast	170	51	30.0	37	72.5
West and Southwest	181	55	30.4	41	74.5
TOTAL	715	216	30.2	160	74.1

Table C-7. All Libraries Surveyed: Size of Group, Sample, Return

	GROUP	SAMPLE		RETURN	
	#	#	% of Group	#	% of Sample
North Atlantic	892	334	37.4	226	67.7
Great Lakes and Plains	923	327	35.4	244	74.6
Southeast	889	299	33.6	206	68.9
West and Southwest	783	308	39.3	225	73.1
TOTAL	3,487	1,268	36.4	901	71.1

Appendix D
(1 of 3)

50 East Huron Street
Chicago, Illinois 60611-2795
USA

Telephone 312 944 6180
Fax 312 440 9374
TDD 312 944 7298
E-mail: ala@ala.org
http://www.ala.org

ALAAmericanLibraryAssocation

April 11, 2003

Dear Colleague:

ALA needs your help in providing information to the library community. The enclosed survey concerns salaries paid to librarians with master's degrees from programs in library and information studies accredited by ALA who hold full-time positions in academic and public libraries. Your institution has been selected as part of a random sample of libraries to receive the enclosed questionnaire. Only summary results will be reported; individual responses will not be identified.

ALA collected and published similar information biennially from 1982 to 1988, and annually since 1989. The results of these surveys have been useful to librarians applying for positions, to librarians setting salaries, and to many others interested in the compensation of librarians. If you have completed this survey before, please note that the categories are somewhat different. Beginning with the 1999 survey, the categories focus on the nature of responsibility for the work of other staff.

Because your library is one of a scientifically selected sample, your response is essential to the success of the survey. As an indication of our thanks for your help, all participants are entitled to a 25% discount on the price of the report. (Mention this entitlement when you place an order. The report will be published in September 2003.) If your staff is very large and this form is difficult to use, please contact Mary Jo Lynch using one of the methods given below. We want your response and will work with you to make use of whatever data you can provide.

Please complete the questionnaire and return it in the enclosed self-addressed, postage-paid envelope. Please return it as soon as possible, but no later than May 2, 2003. If you have questions about the survey, please contact Mary Jo Lynch, Director, ALA Office for Research and Statistics at 1-800-545-2433, ext. 1-4273 or mlynch@ala.org.

Thank you very much for your cooperation.

Sincerely yours,

Keith Michael Fiels
Executive Director
American Library Association

KMF/kdb

P.S. In order to ensure the validity of the survey results, reminders will be sent to nonrespondents.

However, we would rather spend the postage money on other services. Please help our budget by returning this form promptly.

Appendix D
(2 of 3)

50 East Huron Street
Chicago, Illinois 60611-2795
USA

Telephone 312 944 6180
Fax 312 440 9374
TDD 312 944 7298
E-mail: ala@ala.org
http://www.ala.org

ALAAmericanLibraryAssocation

April 11, 2003

Dear Colleague:

ALA needs your help in providing information to the library community. The enclosed survey concerns salaries paid to librarians with master's degrees from programs in library and information studies accredited by ALA who hold full-time positions in academic and public libraries. ALA collected and published similar information biennially from 1982 to 1988, and annually since 1989. The results of these surveys have been useful to librarians applying for positions, to librarians setting salaries, and to many others interested in the compensation of librarians. Only summary results are reported; individual responses are not identified.

Each year the survey form is sent to a sample of public libraries serving populations of 25,000 or more. All public libraries serving 500,000 or more are included because they employ such a large number of professional librarians. Your library is one of that group and we especially value your response. Since we know it is sometimes difficult for larger libraries to respond, we invite you to contact the survey director, Dr. Mary Jo Lynch, if you have any questions or problems. You can contact her by phone (800-545-2433 ext. 4273), email (mlynch@ala.org), or fax (312-280-4392). We want your response and will work with you to make use of whatever data you can provide.

Please complete the questionnaire and return it in the enclosed self-addressed, postage-paid envelope. Please return it as soon as possible, but no later than May 2, 2003. As an indication of our thanks for your help, all participants are entitled to a 25% discount on the price of the report. (Mention this entitlement when you place an order. The report will be published in September 2003.)

Thank you very much for your cooperation.

Sincerely yours,

Keith Michael Fiels
Executive Director
American Library Association

KMF/kdb

P.S. In order to ensure the validity of the survey results, reminders will be sent to nonrespondents. However, we would rather spend the postage money on other services. Please help our budget by returning this form promptly.

50 East Huron Street
Chicago, Illinois 60611-2795
USA

Telephone 312 944 6180
Fax 312 440 9374
TDD 312 944 7298
E-mail: ala@ala.org
http://www.ala.org

ALAAmericanLibraryAssocation

May 9, 2003

Dear Colleague:

A copy of the enclosed "Survey of Librarian Salaries, 2003" was sent to you on April 11th, along with a letter signed by me and with a postage-paid reply envelope. Since we have not yet received a response, we are sending another copy of the form and another reply envelope.

Because you are one of a scientifically selected sample receiving this questionnaire, your response is essential to the success of the study. Accordingly, we are extending the deadline to May 30, 2003 and would appreciate a response by that date. If you have questions or problems with the form, please contact Mary Jo Lynch, Director, ALA Office for Research and Statistics at 1-800-545-2433, ext. 1-4273 or mlynch@ala.org.

Thank you very much for your cooperation.

Sincerely yours,

Keith Michael Fiels
Executive Director
American Library Association

KMF/kdb

P.S. If you have already returned the questionnaire, please disregard this reminder.

Appendix E

AMERICAN LIBRARY ASSOCIATION

SURVEY OF LIBRARIAN SALARIES, 2003

- This survey requests annual salaries paid to full-time professional librarians, i.e., persons who have master's degrees from programs in library and information studies accredited by the ALA.

- It is our expectation that each full-time professional librarian on your library's staff will fit into one of the six categories on this survey. Therefore, salaries for all full-time professional librarians should be reported.

- Please report the actual salary paid to each full-time person in the categories below as of April 1, 2003. Do not include benefits.

- If it is easier for you to use separate sheets of paper or attach a computer printout, please feel free to do so. Also, if you have more employees than the number of spaces provided in a given section, please list additional salaries on a separate piece of paper, and label it with the appropriate category from the survey form.

- If two or more persons in a category have the same annual salary, you need not write the salary more than once. **Instead** indicate the number of persons receiving the particular amount. (e.g., 2@$37,500).

SPECIAL NOTE FOR ACADEMIC LIBRARIES:

- If an incumbent is considered full-time but works LESS than a 12-month year (including vacation), please report the salary and circle the appropriate number of months (9 or 10) for which the salary is paid. The numbers are on the form to the right of each salary line.

- If services are contributed (i.e., institution pays some expenses or an honorarium but not a true salary), please do not list the incumbent.

PART I. SALARIES PAID TO BEGINNING LIBRARIANS

In the last six months did you hire, for full-time work, one or more persons who have master's degrees from programs in library and information studies accredited by ALA but no professional experience after receiving the degree?

Yes   1 (PLEASE LIST ANNUAL SALARIES BELOW)

No   2 (PLEASE CONTINUE THE SURVEY)

_____9/10   _____9/10   _____9/10   _____9/10

_____9/10   _____9/10   _____9/10   _____9/10

Note: Do not repeat these salaries elsewhere on this form.

PART II. SALARIES PAID TO EXPERIENCED LIBRARIANS

Director/Dean* :

List salary of chief officer of the library or library system.

Annual Salary_____ 9/10

* Report only full-time staff *with master's degrees from programs in library and information studies accredited by ALA.*

*Deputy/Associate/Assistant Director** :

List annual salaries of persons who report to the Director and manage major aspects of the library operation (e.g., technical services, public services, collection development, systems/automation).

_____9_10	_____9_10	_____9_10	_____9_10
_____9_10	_____9_10	_____9_10	_____9_10

Department Heads/Coordinators/Senior Managers:*

List annual salaries of persons who supervise one or more professional librarians*.

_____9_10	_____9_10	_____9_10	_____9_10
_____9_10	_____9_10	_____9_10	_____9_10
_____9_10	_____9_10	_____9_10	_____9_10
_____9_10	_____9_10	_____9_10	_____9_10
_____9_10	_____9_10	_____9_10	_____9_10

Managers/Supervisors of support staff:*

List annual salaries of persons who supervise support staff in any part of the library but do <u>not</u> supervise professional librarians.

_____9_10	_____9_10	_____9_10	_____9_10
_____9_10	_____9_10	_____9_10	_____9_10
_____9_10	_____9_10	_____9_10	_____9_10
_____9_10	_____9_10	_____9_10	_____9_10

* Report only full-time staff *with master's degrees from programs in library and information studies accredited by ALA*. Do not repeat salaries from Part 1.

Librarians who do not supervise:

List annual salaries of full-time staff with master's degrees from programs in library and information studies accredited by ALA who were not reported earlier and who have no supervisory responsibilities.

9 _____10	9 _____10	9 _____10	9 _____10
9 _____10	9 _____10	9 _____10	9 _____10
9 _____10	9 _____10	9 _____10	9 _____10
9 _____10	9 _____10	9 _____10	9 _____10
9 _____10	9 _____10	9 _____10	9 _____10
9 _____10	9 _____10	9 _____10	9 _____10

PART III. SUPPLEMENTARY QUESTIONS

Please circle the appropriate code numbers below to indicate what benefits your library provides and which staff are eligible. Use your own definitions of full-time and part-time. Do not report benefits that are for the director only as determined by contract negotiations.

	Professional Staff		Support Staff		Not
	Full-time	Part-time	Full-time	Part-time	provided
Health insurance	1	2	3	4	5
Dental insurance	1	2	3	4	5
Life insurance	1	2	3	4	5
Vision insurance	1	2	3	4	5
Disability insurance	1	2	3	4	5
Prescription insurance	1	2	3	4	5
Vacation	1	2	3	4	5
Sick leave	1	2	3	4	5
Personal days	1	2	3	4	5
Bereavement leave	1	2	3	4	5
Pension	1	2	3	4	5
Retirement savings	1	2	3	4	5
Training & education	1	2	3	4	5

	Professional Staff		Support Staff		Not provided
	Full-time	Part-time	Full-time	Part-time	
Tuition reimbursement	1	2	3	4	5
Credit union	1	2	3	4	5
Professional memberships	1	2	3	4	5
Transportation subsidies	1	2	3	4	5
Child care	1	2	3	4	5
Elder care	1	2	3	4	5
Long-term care	1	2	3	4	5

Other (*please specify benefit & circle appropriate codes*)

_____	1	2	3	4	
_____	1	2	3	4	

Name and title of respondent*: _____

Telephone number: _____

Fax Number: _____   **E-mail address:** _____

* Neither libraries nor individuals will be identified in the report of this survey. The name of your library is given on the last page so that we can avoid sending reminders to libraries that respond. The name, phone, fax, and email address of the person responding are requested because we may need to contact him or her if we have questions about this return.

THANK YOU VERY MUCH! *Please return by May 2, 2003 in the enclosed postage paid envelope.* If you lose the reply envelope, please send the form to:

Library Research Center
University of Illinois at Urbana-Champaign
501 East Daniel Street
Champaign Illinois 61820

Appendix F

Salaries Paid for Less Than a Twelve Month Year in Academic Libraries

Instructions on the questionnaire told the respondent: If the incumbent works **less** than a 12-month year (including vacation), please report the salary and circle the appropriate number of months (9 or 10) for which the salary is paid. A program was written to prorate these salaries to their twelve month equivalents for the purpose of reporting results of this survey. Table F was created to show how often this process was necessary. The first column shows the total from tables in this 2003 report. The second column shows how many were reported as being for nine months and the third column shows the percentage of incumbents in the category (position/type of library) which that number represents. The following columns repeat that pattern for positions reported as being for ten months and then for a combination of nine and ten month salaries.

Table F.

Salaries Paid for Less Than a 12-month Year in Academic Libraries							
	ALL INCUMBENTS	9-MONTH		10-MONTH*		9 AND 10 MONTH	
POSITION AND TYPE OF LIBRARY	#	#	%	#	%	#	%
Director							
Two-year college	118	8	6.8	2	1.7	10	8.5
Four-year college	108	1	<1	1	<1	2	1.9
University	149	0	0.0	0	0.0	0	0.0
Deputy/Associate/Assistant Directors							
Two-year college	57	3	5.3	1	1.8	4	7.0
Four-year college	72	0	0.0	5	6.9	5	6.9
University	325	2	<1	2	<1	4	1.2
Department Heads/Coordinators/Senior Managers							
Two-year college	47	6	12.8	6	12.8	12	25.5
Four-year college	40	0	0.0	0	0.0	0	0.0
University	291	2	<1	8	2.7	10	3.4
Managers/Supervisors of Support Staff							
Two-year college	82	9	11.0	3	3.7	12	14.6
Four-year college	131	6	4.6	3	2.3	9	6.9
University	425	13	3.1	15	3.5	28	6.6
Librarians who do not supervise							
Two-year college	134	33	24.6	13	9.7	46	34.3
Four-year college	137	4	2.9	9	6.6	13	9.5
University	1,427	41	2.9	19	1.3	60	4.2
Beginning Librarians							
Two-year college	8	2	25.0	0	0.0	2	25.0
Four-year college	21	1	4.8	0	0.0	1	4.8
University	90	0	0.0	1	1.1	1	1.1

* includes 28 11-month salaries (14 in two-year colleges and 10 in four-year colleges.)